How I Found Love Behind the Catcher's Mask

POEMS BY

E. ETHELBERT MILLER

City Point Press

City Point Press

PO Box 2063

Westport CT 06880

www.citypointpress.com

(203) 571-0781

Paperback ISBN 978-1-947951-58-7

eBook ISBN 978-1-947951-59-4

Cover and text design by Barbara Aronica-Buck

Cover photograph of John Roseboro by RLFE Pix / Alamy Stock Photo

Author photo courtesy of Denise King-Miller

This book is dedicated to the
memory of Greg Tate, a literary All-Star.

My wife tells me one day,
"I think you love baseball more than me."
I say, "Well, I guess that's true, but hey,
I love you more than football and hockey."

—Tommy Lasorda

Contents

Acknowledgments xi

Introduction—Merrill Leffler xiii

Mood Indigo 3

Every Buddhist Is a Baseball Player 4

Trade Deadline at the Museum 6

Oranges 7

Baseball Cards 8

Sophisticated Lady 9

Sun Ra Left Me Here Standing in Front of the Sam Gilliam 10

Box Score Sonnet 11

The Sounds of the Game 12

Yoga 13

Radio 14

Wild Pitch 15

Walkin' 16

How I Found Love Behind the Catcher's Mask 17

Losing the Lead and One's Children 18

The Black Sox Scandal 19

Chicago 20

Looking for Sidney Bechet 21

Emmett Ashford 22

Poem for Glenn Burke 23

Carl Mays 24

Jimmy Piersall 25

Ken Griffey Sr. 26

Poem for Stacey Abrams 27

Joe DiMaggio 28

It's Either Baseball or Free Jazz 29

Walking Man 30

Trapped Inside the Glove: The American Pitch 31

Baseball Meditation 32

Inside the Park 33

The Changeup 34

Scouting Report 35

Haiti 36

Runners 37

Pine Tar 38

Beanball #2 39

Death of a Ball Player in 9 Innings 40

The Game 43

The Daily News 44

Beer 45

The Haiku Fan 46

The Losing Streak 47

The Slump 48

The Standings 49

The Walk Off 50

The Shooting 51

Just Be Young for Me 52

I Feel 53

Her 54

Hospice 55

A League of Their Own 56

The Things We Leave Behind 57

Querido Clemente 58

Acknowledgments

I would first like to thank David Wilk who keeps my poems on the field and not sitting on the bench.

This third book of my baseball trilogy is possible because of my literary assistant Kirsten Porter. She continues to bless my life by making sure my work is properly dressed before going outside.

I want to thank members of the Pandemic Baseball Book Club, especially Jason Turbow, for building a literary ballpark and letting me run around the bases.

Finally, I want to thank Sam Mondry-Cohen for being a fan of my work. Writers need fans as much as baseball players do.

I love language. I love the game that often translates into love.

Introduction

With the publication of *How I Found Love Behind the Catcher's Mask,* E. Ethelbert Miller's trilogy of baseball poetry books is now complete. Following the tradition of the first book in the collection, *If God Invented Baseball,* and the second book, *When Your Wife Has Tommy John Surgery,* this final book is a celebration of Miller's love of baseball. And yet, the poems that make up these marvelously inventive and richly evocative books are not about baseball in and of itself. Elements of the game are throughout the trilogy—pitching, hitting, baserunning, baseball's artful language, but baseball is more often the springboard for getting poems into play. These improvisational poems may start with baseball, but they move into explorations of subjects ranging widely and randomly from one to another: childhood, youth, love, desire, marriage, divorce, art, music, politics, hatred, racism. The stuff of American culture!

In Miller's trilogy, baseball provides the most unique framing of any modernist work I know —not a structural framing but a linguistic one. The references to baseball give a sense of the connectedness of the 150 mostly short poems in these books that are related to each other through the recurring allusions. For those who know the game and its artful "grammar," the allusions add dimensions of poetic richness and meaning.

Take the title poem, for example, in which the catcher speaking in first-person is squatting behind home plate, Buddha-like. His job: protect the plate and give the pitcher secretive signs on what pitch to throw next, fastball, curve, change-up, slider . . . The operative word is *signs*. The catcher is a master of the call, the player in charge of delivering the signs—his decisions are based on many factors. "All my life I've caught hell. / I never wanted to be a catcher," he begins. "Catcher" becomes the springboard for the implicit subjects. The conventional poem might follow with, "When meeting a woman I never know what to do, or say"; but the catcher's "signs" are both literal and metaphoric, with its punning and nuances about the catcher's self-conscious feelings of failure, his despairs, the "I never know what *signs* to put down." If you don't know that catchers give signs to the pitcher on the kind of pitch to throw next, then *signs* may not radiate the nuances of the catcher's complexity of feelings. But for both those who understand the deeper baseball meanings and those who do not, the poem inspires the question—who is this master of the game behind the mask?

> I live a life of blueness.
> Behind my mask a Buddha smile of suffering.
> Before dying it's important to play catch with yourself.
> You don't have to wait for a woman to throw love at you.

In the poignant poem that follows—also written in first person—"Losing the Lead and One's Children," the elements of baseball again serve up a metaphorical richness, the means for enhancing the feelings of a father whose marriage is coming apart:

Somewhere between first and second
the first bad argument begins like a failed
pickoff throw. The marriage fails and then
the children have to dust their clothes off.
The dirt and mud of accusations cover them
like a tarp before a rain delay.

If you've been to a baseball game when rain forces the ground crew to cover the infield with a tarp, the simile at work in these lines takes on great resonance. Meanwhile, "Another woman starts to steal the signs. // . . . When your children cry all night / you know you're losing the lead. / Things are out of control and there's / nowhere to go. You're out at home / watching it all disappear." "Home" in the poem becomes home plate *and* life itself.

The poems highlighting famous baseball players are far more than a celebration of each hailed player's talents on the field; these poems all have to do with admiration and homage for the kind of men they were. In "Emmett Ashford" (1914–1980), for example, we see a glimpse of the first African American umpire in the major leagues as a charismatic figure: "I call balls and strikes the way / John Coltrane plays 'My Favorite Things.'/ Folks come to the game to hear the sound / of my music . . ." Ashford is more than a baseball player, he's a musician. He's a dancer—

If I'm not behind the plate
I'm dancing in the infield calling runners
out and safe like James Brown sliding
across a stage . . .

We also get this look into more than the baseball player, but
the man, too, in "Carl Mays," a submarine pitching fastballer
whose "hard heat" pitch to Ray Chapman on August 16, 1920,
"knocked Chapman down and he fell / below his knees":

I fell much further the day
he died. We both loved baseball . . .

. . .

Sadness left the Polo Grounds that day.
Sadness climbed down from the stands shocked
by what it saw and what one should never see.

That sadness is juxtaposed by "Ken Griffey Sr." and the tender
feelings for his son, both Hall of Famers:

I loved watching my son play
the way he watched me play or when we played together.
Before the love for the game there was family.

And how we loved each other was how we hit
when other men were on base. There were times
when his injuries made me close my eyes.

Three poems: one of joy, one of grief, one of love. And then a kicker! In "Poem for Stacey Abrams," Miller draws on Ricky Henderson, Major League Baseball's recordholder by far for stolen bases, to bring current American politics and culture into the conversation.

> If they accuse you of being a thief
> Steal first, second, and then third.
> You're Rickey Henderson today
> Sliding head first past Ty Cobb
> And voting restrictions in Georgia.

"Steal"—irony of ironies! Just as Abrams's election as governor of Georgia was stolen, steal here turns its meaning around: claim what is rightfully yours. And by implication, ours.

Miller is an intimate observer who sees and feels the anguish of others. There are poems of racism and hatred by an anonymous narrator, as in "Chicago," which comes at us unexpectedly. "Red Summer of 1919. / Before the Black Sox Scandal. // White men throwing stones / not balls at Black people." And then abruptly, a name, one name—it could have been another—"Eugene Williams . . . // Drowning like a player caught/ in a run down . . ." Run down. If you know anything of baseball, you know a runner trapped between first and second, or second and third, doesn't have a chance. That was Eugene Williams, one of twenty-three dead Black men, trapped in a run down, race riot, not a chance of survival.

Summer of 1919: the year of the infamous game-fixing Black Sox Scandal, where Chicago White Sox players were accused of throwing the World Series against the Cincinnati Reds; the summer as well of some twenty-five race riots throughout the U.S. The poem concludes, "In the alphabet of history / riot comes before scandal." While 1919 in baseball lore is associated with the Black Sox scandal, the understated, bitter last line is miserably ironic, even more so in the context of baseball as the metaphoric "glue" linking all of these poems.

It is a subject Miller comes back to in "Inside the Park":

> During the Great Migration
> Black people headed north
> From the field to the factory.
>
> When your spikes touch third
> you're a good paycheck from
> home.
>
> You're inside the park
> sliding into America
> not knowing if you're out
> or safe.

• • •

What are we to make of this trilogy of baseball books on such wide-ranging subjects—inextricably intertwined with the grammar and spirit of baseball. I have to back up.

Reading the poems of these three books, I thought of Walt Whitman's, "I Hear America Singing," which was published in the original *Leaves of Grass* in 1860, more than 160 years ago. Whitman's poem, one of his most anthologized, gives voice to the "varied carols" he hears, the songs of mechanics, the carpenter, the mason, the boatman, the shoemaker—

> The delicious singing of the mother, or of the young wife at work, or of the girl sewing or washing
> Each singing what belongs to him or her and to none else,
> The day what belongs to the day—at night the party of young fellows, robust, friendly,
> Singing with open mouths their strong melodious songs.

It's a comforting vision of America but hardly relevant today—we don't hear the voices of racism, white supremacy, slavery, the anguish of Blacks and Native Americans, though I must note that Whitman was not deaf to America then—in the 1860 edition of *Leaves of Grass*, his poem "I Sit and Look Out" acknowledged the racial and social disparities of his time:

I SIT and look out upon all the sorrows of the world, and
upon all oppression and shame;

. . .

I observe the slights and degradations cast by arrogant per-
sons upon laborers, the poor, and upon negroes, and the
like;
All these—All the meanness and agony without end, I
sitting, look out upon,
See, hear, and am silent.

Nearly seventy years later in 1926, Langston Hughes
responded to Whitman's poem "I Hear America Singing"
with his perspective, "I, Too":

I, too, sing America:

I am the darker brother.
They send me to eat in the kitchen
When company comes,
But I laugh,
And eat well,
And grow strong.

Less than fifty years later, after the assassination of Malcolm
X and racial violence throughout the country that continues
today, Amiri Baraka changed his name from Leroi Jones, and
published his militant "Black Art." For many, Baraka's poem
became a poetic manifesto of Black separation:

We want a black poem. And a
Black World.
Let the world be a Black Poem
And Let All Black People Speak This Poem
Silently
or LOUD.

The militant voice here is hardly the tone of the poems that make up Miller's trilogy. And while the temper of Miller's work has often been compared to Langston Hughes's poetry, the poems in the baseball trilogy are wholly distinctive in tone. Ethelbert Miller is a Black man in America listening and hearing everyone, and giving them voices. The poems in this trilogy collection are a kaleidoscope of American life in all its tenderness and joys side-by-side with its despairs, its fractures, and disharmonies. It is a grand achievement.

—Merrill Leffler, author of
Mark the Music (poems)
and publisher of Dryad Press

How I Found Love
Behind the
Catcher's Mask

Mood Indigo

How many times has this catcher's mask
been knocked off my head? Oh, those concussions
of love. What is this crazy thing that shakes me now
into a perfectly thrown loneliness?

Every Buddhist Is a Baseball Player

1.
The bullpen is quiet when it laughs at the scoreboard and rubs its
belly

2.
The rally over
You're the third out. Your bat asleep on your shoulder

3.
Falling from the sky
The ball a small moon
Falling like an eclipse into a glove

4.
The designated hitter
Sits in the dugout
Practicing sitting
Meditation

5.
Dirt on a jersey
A symbol
Of devotion
To the
Game

6.

Every Buddhist

A Baseball player

Each breath

A pitch

A catch

A hit

7.

The

Road

From the minors

To the majors

Is the path

Of two

Directions

Trade Deadline at the Museum

I need to finish this next book
A double turning into a trilogy
Time to place more paint in the painting
Take a bigger lead
Add more color and find more words
Death comes with a deadline
I need to join a team where lovers read
Why did O'Hara write about oranges
And not baseballs
Art we play for pleasure not price

Oranges

How many times does the word baseball
appear in this poem? Count the number of lines
in which I removed the word baseball.

Is this still a poem about baseball?
What is a baseball poem?
What is a baseball poem without the word baseball?

I ask O'Hara about oranges and he gives me baseballs.
I decide to write a poem about oranges.

In a supermarket as big as a ball park
I walk down the aisles looking for oranges.

I run into Ginsberg in left field by the oranges.
He chants something about Baraka trying to steal home.
I ask him if he was carrying oranges.

How many Black poets are published every year
because they only write about oranges?

Baseball Cards

Black history was years ahead of us
so when we gathered in the playground
we traded away our baseball cards
with the black faces.

We were blinded by white stars
and even disappointed our West Indian
parents who loved cricket but knew
the man who wore 42.

Integration came to our neighborhood
the day we opened a new pack
of cards and watched the sugar
fall from the gum to our fingers.

Sophisticated Lady

Why did Ellington say music was his mistress
and not baseball?

Somewhere between swing and bebop
Satchel Paige took the mound.

Fingering the keys is as beautiful
as fingering the ball.

Cool Papa Bell believed he was cooler than jazz.
Turn out the lights and grab the bass by the bed.

Did Dizzy Dean ever wear a beret?
Dizzy did.

Sun Ra Left Me Here Standing in Front of the Sam Gilliam

When did I stop warming up, sending poems
to journals, doing workshops, readings
and conferences? When did I no longer write
for the page? Why do I no longer have a desire
to buy a ticket or watch a game?

I pass the metro station that would take me
to the ballpark. I'm in the same train car
as Clay in LeRoi's play The Dutchman.
Lula is sitting next to me. She's the type of woman
who only dates jazz musicians and ballplayers
for money and good seats.

I tell young writers to read box scores
and not the headlines. Romance is like the weather -
difficult to predict and always changing.
Let me live in a small room with a television
and a few more years to live.

Please take my clothes to the cleaners.
Clean my suit before I die.
Baseball has no arms.
It can only hold you for so long.

Box Score Sonnet

I escaped the workshop but not the box score.
There are times when I get tired of describing
what base I'm on. Why I write my name and age
in an empty box? Once an editor took a look
at my manuscript and returned it with strange
markings. I couldn't keep the lineup or narrative
straight or find the correct punctuation
for putouts. I'm old school and only know
baseball shorthand. The box score documents
the facts and ways of losing. One has to ponder
and imagine how a game is won. I believe errors
are impossible when writing a poem. Writing
is all about avoiding mistakes. It's about hitting
and putting words in play.

The Sounds of the Game

It's the only sound you hear
the sound you will remember
the sound before you turn around
and follow the arc, the rainbow of the homer
your gift, your pot of gold, hand given
and gift wrapped to the hitter. The sound
of it, the crack of the bat, the crack
that destroys your life. It's the sound
that leaves you helpless on the mound
staring at the rosin bag wearing a silly
minstrel grin. A grin that will stick to you
and haunt your nights, your lonely silent
nights before the crack of dawn, when
the darkness slowly lifts and still you
cannot hear the sound of anything more
or anything else or anything again.

Yoga

In the early sixties we were young
boys without yoga mats. We had yet to read
Kerouac or Ginsberg. We thought Zen
was a soft drink. We lost our balance
when we tried to be Juan Marichal
or Warren Spahn. We wanted to kick
the stars in the mouth and chase the moon.
We kicked high and threw hard.
If only our parents could afford spikes.
We wanted to be All-Star pitchers
in a league of our own. We went to bed
early in search of dreams and meditation.

Radio

When we were small
we listened to the games on small radios.
In our beds we imagined ourselves in dugouts
instead of darkness. We became the names
we wore on our backs. Our favorite number,
our favorite player, our favorite team. Static
interrupted the games like parents and
pickoffs. Parents afraid we might be losers
if we continued to think life was a game.
The games came from far away. Maybe there
was nothing inside those radios except our
small hearts beating and cheering us on.
What do you think?

Wild Pitch

Your family slips under your glove
Your son rolls past a police car
The ball bounces off the wall behind you
There is nothing you can do

Walkin'

(Miles Davis 1957)

Sometimes when the innings get long
the stories become shorter.

The mind wanders and you find yourself
walkin' beyond first base.

Your relatives try to coach you
back into yourself.

But you're walkin' more these days.
Passing memories and people you

try to love
and remember.

How I Found Love Behind
the Catcher's Mask

All my life I've caught hell.

I never wanted to be a catcher.

When meeting a woman I never know what signs to put down.

I never have enough protection.

Once a girlfriend told me she was pregnant.

She lied but I didn't know it.

A man can only see so much.

I live a life of blueness.

Behind my mask a Buddha smile of suffering.

Before dying it's important to play catch with yourself.

You don't have to wait for a woman to throw love at you.

Losing the Lead and One's Children

Somewhere between first and second
the first bad argument begins like a failed
pickoff throw. The marriage fails and then
the children have to dust their clothes off.
The dirt and mud of accusations cover them
like a tarp before a rain delay.

The inning began as a honeymoon.
A hit here and there. A vacation and job promotion.
A new home before new troubles began.
Another woman starts to steal the signs.

You start to miss your children's games,
birthdays and bedtime stories. You're losing
them to the monster inside yourself.
The hungry thing you can't explain.
The wild thing. The lust and desire.

When your children cry all night
you know you're losing the lead.
Things are out of control and there's
nowhere to go. You're out at home
watching it all disappear.

The Black Sox Scandal

My mother was a mystery to me.
A shoeless woman of secrets and quiet faith.
When she was in the kitchen I could hear
her praying - "Lord, Lord, give me strength."
My mother was born
the year of the Black Sox Scandal.
There are stories about a nurse picking her up
and saying "She will one day give birth to a poet."
"Say it ain't so" my dad cried many years later.
"Say it ain't so."

Chicago

Red Summer of 1919.
Before the Black Sox Scandal.

White men throwing stones
not balls at Black people.

Black people at the beach not
wearing socks or shoes.

Eugene Williams was not a fan
of violence. He was a victim.

Drowning like a player caught
in a run down. Cheated out of his life.

In the alphabet of history
riot comes before scandal.

Looking for Sidney Bechet

One didn't have to live in Boston to believe
in Green Monsters. Every housing project
had a wall haunting our future. The Bronx
was where Black people went after they hit
the number in Harlem. I had an Elston
Howard baseball card but didn't know
he was black behind his catcher's mask.
Howard played for the Yankees and Pumpsie
Green played for the Red Sox. I didn't want
to be either of them. I was a young skinny
kid with a big glove and a kid who never
knew much about Boston except the year
Bill Monbouquette threw a no-hitter
that was almost a perfect game. I liked
the sound of his name because it reminded
me of Paris and a French kiss and maybe
one day a woman would think I was lucky
or had just hit the number and maybe
some French woman might just mistake me
might just mistake me for Sidney Bechet.

Emmett Ashford

(1914–1980)

I call balls and strikes the way
John Coltrane plays "My Favorite Things."
Folks come to the game to hear the sound
of my music. Some batters stand in the box
like bass players who don't know how to play.

If I'm not behind the plate
I'm dancing in the infield calling runners
out and safe like James Brown sliding
across a stage. I've had managers run
from dugouts only to protest and scream

"Please, Please, Please."

Poem for Glenn Burke

Everyone flirts in the game.
You miss the sign to bunt.
You overrun the base.
You watch the ball turn foul
at the last moment.

What does it mean to love the game
and love the man undressing next to you?
What must you be forced to dodge
your entire life?

Somewhere a man wants to touch or trade you.
Some want you out.

Carl Mays

(August 16th 1920)

When the ball rolls towards me I scoop it up
and throw to Wally Pipp at first. It's the natural
thing to do and I've done it many times without
thinking. I would never think about killing
anyone but August 16th is all I think about.

That day I faced shortstop Ray Chapman.
A fast, sweet player who could bunt better
than the best. I threw inside my hard heat -
a pitch that might make a batter sweat, make
them wipe their brow and temple.

The ball knocked Chapman down and he fell
below his knees. I fell much further the day
he died. We both loved baseball. I thought
the ball hit his bat but it hit his head. Our names
now forever linked like cursed lovers.

Sadness left the Polo Grounds that day.
Sadness climbed down from the stands shocked
by what it saw and what one should never see.

Jimmy Piersall

(1929–2017)

Maybe I have fans or just my dad in my head.
What's the difference between being bipolar
and warming up two relievers in the bullpen?
One right. One left.

I love baseball. Sometimes it's a crazy game.
I once had six hits in one.
That day I felt I could never strike out.

I only had a fear of failing and falling again.

Ken Griffey Sr.

Even before my son turned his cap backwards
I wanted to keep him close. Keep an eye on him.
I didn't want to worry beyond the outfield like other fathers.

I loved watching my son play
the way he watched me play or when we played together.
Before the love for the game there was family.

And how we loved each other was how we hit
when other men were on base. There were times
when his injuries made me close my eyes.

But my eyes could never close after seeing the beauty of his swing
or the catches made near the wall.
Baseball was good to us.

History will remember us because we made history.
My son's Hall of Fame smile
another RBI for the record books.

Poem for Stacey Abrams

You're Rickey Henderson today.
You're leading off.
You have power and speed.
You have flex and flair.
You're brash. You're Black.

If they accuse you of being a thief
Steal first, second, and then third.
You're Rickey Henderson today
Sliding head first past Ty Cobb
And voting restrictions in Georgia.

Joe DiMaggio

for M

After just a few years of marriage
We both went hitless and decided to divorce.
It was desirable for both of us.

We had met at Howard and were together
Almost every day we were on campus.
It was a streak we knew one day would end.

Now both in our 7th inning we meet outside
a downtown metro station.
I feel like Joe DiMaggio walking
with Marilyn Monroe.

It's Either Baseball or Free Jazz

Today I ran into Don Cherry.
He had a pocket trumpet in one pocket
and a baseball in the other.
He reminded me that I should be practicing
more. When I write I tend to bounce words
off walls instead of the floor like Pollock.

Cherry once played catch with Coltrane
in that Avant Garde park around 1966.
The same year the Orioles swept the Dodgers
in the World Series and we all thought
it was too much Charlie Haden on bass.

Walking Man

Giacometti in the batter's box.
His back and bat now straight -
Now leaning.

He takes a look at the first
and third base lines.
His eyes draw a line
to the pitcher.

The sculpture of the moment.
The shared air between them.

Trapped Inside the Glove:
The American Pitch

We almost took a hard fast one to the head.

We stumbled out of voting booths as if we had seen a curve.

We avoided the sliders as if they were lies.

We knew what cutters did to our rights.

We lived with the crazy knuckleballs of history.

We kept swinging at the flutter, the rotation of freedom.

Baseball Meditation

one man's fast is another man's slow
                                        —*Amiri Baraka*

Because the game is slow
you have more than enough time
to think about all the black boys
who never made it to first or the bad
boys caught trying to steal second.
The slowness of the game makes
you think of slavery and how slavery
was too long and too slow for history
to forget.

Inside the Park

For a second at second
you glance out at the outfield.

The ball is rolling
still rolling…

You push your head down
and find another way to pump
your legs.

During the Great Migration
Black people headed north
From the field to the factory.

When your spikes touch third
you're a good paycheck from
home.

You're inside the park
sliding into America
not knowing if you're out
or safe.

The Changeup

What is the difference between a changeup and a coup?
Democracy can depart from a hand very fast.
Elections quickly over like fast balls and airplanes
Zooming over the plate..

The changeup is nothing but illusion.
A slow curfew at night.
Too many countries embrace the changeup.
They think it's the surprise that comes with a free press.

The changeup is dress rehearsal for fascism.
Citizens soon find themselves trapped in the hitter's box
Wrapping a baseball bat with a flag.
Running from the field into the stands.
Smashing the scoreboard and changing the score.

Scouting Report

Should we believe Ethel and Julius Rosenberg?
What edge do we get when knowing the pitch?
What signs can we steal and get away with?

During the Cold War even Jackie Robinson stole.
My mother tiptoeing through the 1950 snow
Bringing me home to a cold apartment in the Bronx.

According to FBI scouting reports
Some babies wore red diapers and were breast
Fed by Communists - oh, those naked, nuclear nipples.

Under school desks children cringed and cried
Turning away from windows and the atomic wind
Whistling outside and segregation chasing Emmett boys home.

Haiti

The line keeps moving . . .
Earthquakes, hurricanes, mudslides—every catastrophe known
to the living. Haiti can't find an out
in History's lineup.

The game started with so much promise.
A leadoff revolution in the hemisphere.
A grand slam filled with hope and freedom by Toussaint
who separated from the old French league.

Sadly reality has its own scoreboard and plays by its own rules.
I write to Edwidge Danticat praying her grace might change the
outcome
of this inning. Weren't we once masters of the dew? So much curves
against this country. Many leave and many can't.

Do they still make baseballs in Haiti?

Runners

To run outside the base paths
Is to give the body pleasure.
To be Black, to Frederick Douglass freedom.
We run, in order to run from, to run to.
Where is our place inside this batter's box
Called America?

Pine Tar

Backstage we painted
our faces. Lips red
our black corked faces
wide-eyed, grinning
and slipping. Our lost
souls losing grip on
our dignity. Wrinkles
coming with shame
and pain. Pine tar
sticking to our battered
spines.

Beanball #2

The beanball is a demon.
Depression a night game
with only night. My
crumpled body motionless
by the plate. No hands
to lift me up.

Death of a Ball Player in 9 Innings

Always go to other people's funerals, otherwise they won't come to yours.
—Yogi Berra

I.

It's the game that gives your life meaning.

II.

Parents are shortstops and second basemen.
We confuse them with pitchers and catchers.

III.

To run around the bases is to chase oneself.
Most people play tag with their dreams.
Memory is just a ball in the air.

IV.

The scoreboard is nothing but an obituary.
By the time you reach fifty it's over.
The blues is a rain delay.
A broken guitar won't play in a dugout.

V.

Marriage is an official game.
Too many feel cheated when it ends.
Lies are nothing but confessions.
A curveball is a woman's best friend.
The fastball refuses to walk down the aisle.

VI.

A woman might turn her back to a man on second.
Too many stolen hearts never reach third or home.
If you find yourself in the outfield don't turn around.
There is always a fence in a relationship.
Running into a wall is something else.
Outside church every single woman needs a fan.

VII.

Keep your business in the ball park when you stand.
Gossip always has a high batting average.
The bullpen is not a bar.
When you hear your wife whispering check the number of outs.
Love never lasts in the late innings unless you're lucky.
Use the right bat if you can't find the right glove.
A foul ball is nothing but desire getting in the way.

VIII.

Sex is often a hitting streak coming to an end.
Never mistake a lover for a rally.
Lose your cap but don't lose your pants.
If you have to steal signs you will never fall in love.
Divorce never makes it into the last inning.
If you're on first ask your therapist how you got there.
If you're on second don't look over your shoulder.
If you need a third beer you might never get to third.

IX.

Death is a poor leadoff hitter.
Too many strike out before the funeral.
Amazing Grace is better than the National Anthem.
Learn to smile during the eulogy.
Be sure they get your stats right.
Remember there are no more home games.
The Devil is a closer.
Jesus prayed for extra innings when he was on the cross.
There is only Ascension after baseball.

The Game

The stadiums and ballparks
are empty. There are no fans.
Not even God.

What is the purpose of life
if there are no games
or opponents to defeat?

Why run or score?
Meaning is an exit into existence.
Dying is a spectator sport.

The Daily News

It's when the relief pitchers die
You know your days are no longer
As long as your innings

You read obituaries like box scores
Knowing someone will one day see yours
Forgetting your team and the position you played

You tried to live your life pitch by pitch
But the ballpark becomes dark
The field empty

The grass a quiet cemetery green

Beer

When I arrive at the ballpark
no one recognizes me. They ignore my uniform.
There is no number on my back. I'm just a number.
This—a part-time job.

I sell beer. I carry beer. I walk up and down
yelling "beer." "Beer here, beer."
When I see a raised hand or hear "Beer here"
I rest my load, my rack of beer.

It's the crowd's thirst that pays my bills.
I could make more money if I sold my blood.
But who would drink my sweat -
my blood like they drink this beer?

Who would catch me if I stumbled?
Who would love this foul ball?

The Haiku Fan

here at the ballpark
players flower in the green
hotdogs beer and sun

The Losing Streak

It happens when it happens.
It might never end.
You arrive at the ballpark
Knowing you might lose again.
There are no explanations
Or bullpen saviors.
There are only double-plays,
Walks with three runners on,
Dropped balls and wild pitches.
Everything begins to lose its grip.
Game after game the same.
The losing is a long sentence in a novel
Or a long sentence in a court.
Fans judge and blame the manager.
Out with the play-calling, strange lineups
And not changing pitchers.
A losing streak is a hungry bastard
Feeding on cold hot dogs and warm beer.

The Slump

Every slump begins with superstition
and a girl you want to date.
You do everything but everything
seems to be going wrong.
You start talking to yourself
because the ball keeps turning its back.
You're swinging and calling every day.
Somewhere there's a sweet spot
in your lumber and some hits in your bat.
You just don't know where love is.

The Standings

for Sam

In late August you begin each game
waiting for the pitching change, the blown save,
the error in the infield or outfield. It's not that
summer is long, the losing is longer. Your team
is sweating in the standings, drowning in their
mistakes. Last place is the last thing fans
want to see. Not enough people to do the wave.
Too few to cheer. Next year things could be worse
or they could be the same, they won't be better.
You think of tearing your uniform off and streaking
across the field. But where would you run to?
When you're in last place there's no exit to first.
You're caught in a cafe talking analytics with Camus
and Sartre. What is the meaning of baseball?
Does God or first place even exist?

The Walk Off

When the bat kisses the ball
you know it's farewell.

You stand in the box
watching your life

fade into the
night sky.

The Shooting

You think drive by when you
clutch your hamstring, the pain
makes you stop between first
and second. You crawl back
on two legs before you bend
over at first. The coach puts
his arm around you and signals
for the trainer. You start to count
the games you're gonna miss.
Soon your leg will be up in the air.

Just Be Young for Me

The speed of your throws goes first.
You move slower too.
The location of your throws
suddenly gone. You can't remember
Where the plate is. You can't remember
Home. The sky darkens and it has
Nothing to do with rain. You kick
The dirt around the mound and
Think of memories. There is nothing
Left in your arm. But your heart is
Strong, it is beating and you're finally
Learning how to live without caring
About the errors or the score. You catch
Your breath, adjust your belt and cap.
Just breathe now baby. Just breathe.

I Feel

I feel
Sometimes somewhere someone

Is reading a newspaper
With my obituary in it.

The news of the day is fiction.
Do you believe the good life is possible

On earth?

Only the sports page
Lists winners and losers.

Everyday another game is played
With or without you.

Records are meant to be broken
No matter how well you dance.

Her

At her funeral
it was mentioned
during the eulogy
that she was
a great softball
player on a great
softball team

It was her boyfriend
who made her quit
because he thought
her playing on the team
would make her a
lesbian

A ball can do that
to a woman. She can fall
in love with its softness
and how it curves

One never knows when
a woman might leave home
with a bat in her hands
and swing at the world

Hospice

You think about the sacrifice bunt
and how leaving is nothing but letting go.

You shorten the hold on your bat.
Stare God in the face—and breathe.

A League of Their Own

Did Gertrude Stein ever pitch to Yogi Berra?

Language is the perfect game.

Like a rose people no longer buy because it's too popular.

Gertrude and Yogi and Yogi and Gertrude walk into a ballpark.

When does one turn a joke into a poem?

If you can't make it to the majors be a magician.

Watch me make words dis...

The Things We Leave Behind

Bat

Ball

Glove

Cap

Helmet

Rosin bag

Batting gloves

Pine Tar

Cleats

Wrist Bands

Sunglasses

Jersey

Socks

Pants

And the Things We Take

Bruises

Scars

The love of the game

Querido Clemente

(December 31, 1972)

Your death the other earthquake.
The plane crash a reminder that miracles
disappear. You left us on the edge
of December—the last day of the year.

From Puerto Rico to Nicaragua
we stared into an empty ocean filling it
with our tears. Lost was our beautiful
Pirate, our shining jewel who played
right field with amazing grace.

Your throws - arrows cutting through
the space forever somewhere. Your
running the bases with dignity helped
us all hold our heads up and count
the stars in Spanish.